For the Teacher

This reproducible study guide to use in conjunction with the novel *Of Mice and Men* consists of lessons for guided reading. Written in chapter-by-chapter format, the guide contains a synopsis, pre-reading activities, vocabulary and comprehension exercises, as well as extension activities to be used as follow-up to the novel.

In a homogeneous classroom, whole class instruction with one title is appropriate. In a heterogeneous classroom, reading groups should be formed: each group works on a different novel at its own reading level. Depending upon the length of time devoted to reading in the classroom, each novel, with its guide and accompanying lessons, may be completed in three to six weeks.

Begin using NOVEL-TIES for reading development by distributing the novel and a folder to each child. Distribute duplicated pages of the study guide for students to place in their folders. After examining the cover and glancing through the book, students can participate in several pre-reading activities. Vocabulary questions should be considered prior to reading a chapter; all other work should be done after the chapter has been read. Comprehension questions can be answered orally or in writing. The classroom teacher should determine the amount of work to be assigned, always keeping in mind that readers must be nurtured and that the ultimate goal is encouraging students' love of reading.

The benefits of using NOVEL-TIES are numerous. Students read good literature in the original, rather than in abridged or edited form. The good reading habits, formed by practice in focusing on interpretive comprehension and literary techniques, will be transferred to the books students read independently. Passive readers become active, avid readers.

SYNOPSIS

Of Mice and Men is a short work of fiction in which the central characters are two rootless and homeless men, Lennie Small and George Milton. When the story opens the two men are walking to a ranch to work as hired hands. Their real goal is to earn enough money to buy themselves a small farm. If America is truly the land of opportunity, then, Lennie and George reason, they should be able to earn a decent living and buy a piece of the American dream. Whether or not Lennie and George are destined to fulfill their dream is always in doubt, because Lennie, who is developmentally retarded, has a history of violent, though unintentional, behavior.

When they arrive at the ranch, it becomes clear to George that he must protect Lennie from a variety of potential dangers: from the boss's son Curley, a former boxer who instigates trouble wherever he goes; from Curley's wife, the only woman on the ranch, who has a tendency to flirt with other men and thereby excite Curley's fury; and most of all, from the indiscriminate sharing of their dream with those who could harm them. George instructs Lennie that in case of danger, he should run away and hide in a predetermined spot. There, George will join him, and they can start all over again in a new place.

Lennie and George inspire a naïve hope in some of their fellow workers who hope to share in the dream of a farm of their own. Lennie offers Candy, a disabled older man, the opportunity to live on the ranch with him and George. He offers the same hope to Crooks, a crippled black stable hand.

Lennie accidentally kills a puppy given to him by one of the other ranch hands. Curley's wife walks in upon a confused Lennie trying to understand the death of his pup. Before long, her playful invitation to Lennie to stroke her silky hair excites him. He grips her too hard, causing her to scream. In fear and bewilderment he tightens his grip and shakes her so violently that he breaks her neck. Lennie remembers George's warning and runs away to wait for George at their predetermined place in the woods.

When George and Candy come upon the scene of the crime, they immediately understand what has happened. Curley arrives and turns the search party for Lennie into a lynching party. George joins the men in their search for his friend. When he finds Lennie, he very gently rehearses the words to their favorite fantasy about buying the farm and tending rabbits, even as he aims a gun at the base of Lennie's skull. He pulls the trigger himself to spare his friend a more brutal death.

ABOUT THE AUTHOR

John (Ernst) Steinbeck was born on February 27, 1902 in Salinas, California. He was the third of four children born to Olive Hamilton Steinbeck and John Ernst Steinbeck, Jr.

In 1919, the young Steinbeck graduated from Salinas High School and began his undergraduate studies at Stanford University. For six years he alternately studied and worked odd jobs to finance his education, but never earned a degree. Steinbeck tried writing fiction at college, and made a serious attempt to pursue writing as a career. Upon leaving Stanford in 1926, Steinbeck took a berth on a freighter to New York City, but after an unsuccessful year, he returned to the West Coast.

In 1929, Steinbeck published his first novel, *Cup of Gold*. But it wasn't until the publication of *Tortilla Flat* in 1935 that he had his first literary success. In 1937, Steinbeck published "a tricky little thing designed to teach [him] to write for the theatre." This novel, the first draft of which was partially eaten by Steinbeck's setter pup, was *Of Mice and Men*. The desired result (creating a theatrical piece) was achieved when this novella was produced as a play and won the Drama Critics' Circle Award.

John Steinbeck was a prolific author who perfected his craft by writing in many different genres: he was a war correspondent, wrote novels, novellas, short stories, nonfiction, and screenplays. He is, however, best remembered for the Pulitzer-Prize-winning *The Grapes of Wrath*, a realistic and unflinching portrayal of the plight of migratory workers in Depression-era America.

Works by John Steinbeck include: *Tortilla Flat* (1935); *In Dubious Battle* (1936); *Of Mice and Men* (1937); *The Grapes of Wrath* (1939); *The Moon is Down* (1942); *Cannery Row* (1945); *The Pearl* (1947); *The Red Pony* (1949); *The Wayward Bus* (1947); *Burning Bright* (1950); *East of Eden* (1952); *The Winter of Our Discontent* (1961).

He also wrote four screenplays: *The Pearl* (1948); *The Red Pony* (1949); *Forgotten Village* (1941); *Viva Zapata!* (1952).

John Steinbeck died in 1968.

BACKGROUND INFORMATION

The Great Depression

The Great Depression refers to the severe worldwide economic crisis, which was precipitated by the Wall Street stock market crash in October 1929. At that time millions of dollars of stock were subject to panic selling in a matter of hours. This forced the closure of many banks whose reserves were involved in stock speculation. Suddenly, the investments of millions of people were lost. In the United States businesses closed, people lost their homes, and by 1933, sixteen million people, or one-third of the labor force, were unemployed. Complete recovery from the Depression came only with the heavy defense spending of World War II in the 1940s.

The Salinas Valley

The Salinas Valley in the Central Coast region of California lies along the Salinas River between the Gabilan Range and the Santa Lucia Range. The city of Salinas was established after Mexico seceded from Spain in 1822 and began granting rancho lands. Named for a nearby salt marsh, Salinas became the seat of Monterey County in 1872 and incorporated in 1874.

Agriculture dominates the economy of the valley. In particular, a large majority of the salad greens consumed in the U.S. are grown within this region. For this reason, the Salinas Valley is known as "The Salad Bowl of the World."

Born in the Salinas Valley in 1902, John Steinbeck spent many years roaming the hills and valleys that were used in his stories. He did not only know what the Salinas Valley looked like; he also knew how the people who lived there were treated. Working many odd jobs, Steinbeck was able to incorporate his experiences into those of the characters in his books.

PRE-READING ACTIVITIES

1. Preview the book by reading the title and the author's name and by looking at the illustration on the cover. What do you think this book will be about? Where and when does it take place? Are you familiar with any other works by the same author?

2. **Social Studies Connection:** This novel takes place in the 1930s, a time known as the Great Depression. Read the Background Information on the Great Depression on page three of this study guide and do some additional research to learn how the lives of farmers and farm workers were affected. Also, learn about migrant farm workers. Then discuss the following questions with your classmates:
    *   In what parts of the United States might you find migrant workers?
    *   What were the living conditions of migrant farm workers during the 1930s?
    *   Are conditions the same or different for migrant workers today?

3. **Social Studies Connection:** Find the state of California on a map of the United States. Then, locate the following places:
    *   Salinas River
    *   Gabilan Mountains
    *   Salinas Valley
    *   Soledad

4. Read the Background Information on the Salinas Valley on page three of this study guide. Then try to locate pictures of farmland and farm conditions in California, particularly in the Salinas Valley, during the 1930s and today. Compare and contrast the same area over time and discuss the changes with your class.

5. Read the poem "To a Mouse," by Robert Burns. Interpret the lines, "The best-laid schemes o' mice an' men / Gang aft a-gley" (often go awry). Has there been a situation in your life that could be an example of this quotation? Write about such a time. When you complete the book, tell why you think Steinbeck chose the title *Of Mice and Men* for this work of fiction.

6. Define and discuss mental retardation. Differentiate between functional retardates and those who must be institutionalized. Have you had personal contact with either group? What are some of the popular misconceptions about mental retardation? How can the functional retardate be helped to enjoy a good life?

7. **Cooperative Learning Activity:** In a cooperative learning group, read aloud excerpts from several Steinbeck novels. What are the major characteristics of his writing style? What are the qualities of his style that have made him such a compelling writer of fiction?

8. Do you think it is ever justified for one human being to take the life of another? Use this question as the touchstone for a debate, and make a list of any conditions under which homicide might be justifiable. Also, discuss the controversial concept of "mercy killing."

9. Read "About the Author" on page two of this study guide. As you read the book, determine how John Steinbeck's life and the place he lived affected his work as a writer.

PAGES 1–16 [Penguin Edition]

Vocabulary: Draw a line from each word on the left to its definition on the right. Then use the numbered words to fill in the blanks in the sentences below.

1. recumbent   a. gazed at attentively
2. lumbered   b. in a lordly or arrogant manner
3. emerge   c. position suggestive of resting
4. morosely   d. come forth into view
5. contemplated   e. sad or gloomy
6. imperiously   f. in a downcast manner
7. dejected   g. moved clumsily, as if burdened

. . . .

1. Sharon stared _____ at the broken vase, afraid to tell her mother that she was the one who had broken it.

2. As we gazed at the wetlands bordering the creek, we saw a heron _____ from the grass and fly overhead.

3. Albert became _____ when he realized that he was the only one in his group of friends who would not be going away for the summer.

4. When Justine first got her cast removed, she _____ about as if her leg were still encased in plaster.

5. The teacher _____ the papers before her with care; she wanted to make very sure that the two students who sat next to each other had not copied each other's work.

6. Accustomed to ordering her servants about, Mrs. Stoddard was unprepared for criticism when she spoke _____ to her fellow volunteers.

7. The doctor eased his patient into a(n) _____ position before beginning the examination.

Questions:

1. How is Lennie characterized when he is first introduced? What leads to this impression?

2. What is the relationship between Lennie and George?

3. Why are Lennie and George traveling?

4. Why are Lennie and George forced to lead a nomadic life?

Pages 1–16 (cont.)

5. What evidence suggests that Lennie might behave violently? What motivates Lennie to behave this way?

6. What evidence suggests that George is not optimistic about the duration of his new job?

Questions for Discussion:

1. Read the first two paragraphs of the book. Why do you think the author juxtaposes an idyllic description of the landscape with a statement concerning the people who traverse this place?

2. Why do you think Lennie chose to carry a dead mouse in his pocket? Was George justified in taking it from Lennie?

3. Do you think that George means it when he says to Lennie, "God you're a lot of trouble . . . . I could get along so easy and so nice if I didn't have you on my tail"?

4. Do you think George believes that his dream for the future will come true? Why does he repeatedly tell the story of his dream to Lennie?

Literary Device:

I. *Motif*—A motif is a term for an often-repeated character, incident, or idea in literature. Steinbeck repeats several ideas throughout these pages and then throughout the book. These motifs help define character and provide a cohesive unity to the plot. In a chart such as the one below, begin a list of motifs and keep track of their reappearance throughout the novel. The first one has been done for you.

Motif	Example	Page Numbers
rabbits	Lennie remembers the rabbits and forgets everything else about their last experience	4, 5

II. *Personification*—Personification is a figure of speech in which an author grants human qualities to nonhuman objects. For example:

> Evening of a hot day started the little wind to moving among the leaves. The shade climbed up the hills toward the top.

What two objects are being personified?

_____

Why do you think the author used this device?

_____

_____

Pages 1–16 (cont.)

Literary Element: Author's Style

Notice the great difference between the language of the narrated passages and the dialogue between characters in the novel. The vocabulary and level of sophistication seems radically different. Do you think this is purposeful or accidental? What is the effect of this difference? In what ways is this novel written as though it were a play?

_____

_____

_____

_____

Writing Activity:

We are given clues to the feelings of George and Lennie through the narration and through the dialogue. Imagine you are one of these characters and write a journal entry describing your situation and your hopes and dreams for the future.

PAGES 17–37

Vocabulary: Use the context to determine the meaning of the underlined word in each of the following sentences. Then compare your definition with a dictionary definition.

1. Although the entertainer may <u>scoff</u> at the award publicly, he is really very proud to have received it.

    Your definition _____

    Dictionary definition _____

2. The flags in the harbor <u>ominously</u> warned sailors that they should remain ashore because a storm was coming.

    Your definition _____

    Dictionary definition _____

3. The dog looked <u>plaintively</u> at its master for a bowl of water to quench its thirst.

    Your definition _____

    Dictionary definition _____

4. Despite his ragged clothes, the stranger entered the room, moving with a <u>majesty</u> only seen in kings and their courtiers.

    Your definition _____

    Dictionary definition _____

5. The young candidate was so serious and firm of purpose that his presence produced a <u>profound</u> silence whenever he began to speak.

    Your definition _____

    Dictionary definition _____

6. Being very shy, I allowed my friend to <u>precede</u> me to the party, knowing I would be more comfortable finding a familiar face.

    Your definition _____

    Dictionary definition _____

7. I rubbed <u>liniment</u> on my sprained ankle to ease the pain until I could visit the doctor.

    Your definition _____

    Dictionary definition _____

Pages 17–37 (cont.)

Questions:

1. Why is Crooks at the lowest level in the bunkhouse hierarchy?
2. How does Candy's name reflect his character?
3. Why is the boss suspicious of George's protectiveness of Lennie?
4. Why does George lie about the cause of Lennie's mental deficiency?
5. Why might Curley pose a threat to George and Lennie?
6. Why does Curley's wife pose a threat to George and Lennie?
7. Who stands at the top of the bunkhouse hierarchy? How has he achieved his status?
8. What does Slim's remark, "Ain't many guys travel around together," suggest about the world they know? What different implication does Slim's remark have than the boss's remark, even though the words are the same?

Questions for Discussion:

1. Do you think George is justified in not telling others the truth about Lennie's mental deficiency?
2. What do you think the author meant when referring to Slim that "his ear heard more than was said to him"?
3. How has Steinbeck created a growing sense of tension and an increasingly ominous tone even though nothing tragic has yet occurred? What does this lead the reader to expect? How do you think the tension will be resolved?
4. How has each of the important motifs introduced in the first section been repeated in the second section (e.g. rabbits, George's need for a place of his own, etc.)?
5. Why do you think the author referred to Slim's drowning of his dog's pups? What moral judgment should be drawn from this incident?

Literary Device: Foreshadowing

Foreshadowing in literature refers to the clues or hints an author provides to suggest what will happen later on in the novel. What might be foreshadowed when George reminds Lennie about their emergency meeting place?

_____

_____

Writing Activity:

In many ways, Steinbeck's short novel *Of Mice and Men* is written as though it were a play. The "stage" is carefully set before action or dialogue begins and each "player" is vividly described. The story moves forward more through dialogue than through narration. Reread the beginning of this section and write a stage version of this part of the novel. Indicate setting, include some character description, and write dialogue.

PAGES 38 - 65

Vocabulary: Antonyms are words with opposite meanings. Draw a line from each word in column A to its antonym in column B. Then use the words in column A to fill in the blanks in the sentences below.

A	B
1. confident	a. frankness
2. entranced	b. repel
3. reprehensible	c. accidental
4. conceal	d. apprehensive
5. sarcasm	e. bored
6. deliberate	f. praiseworthy
7. attract	g. reveal
8. cautious	h. reckless

. . . .

1. At a busy intersection, you must be _____ when you cross the street.

2. The young child gazed at the puppies, _____ by their small, furry bodies.

3. The policeman's _____ was obvious when he said to the driver, "Do you think you were driving on the Indianapolis Speedway"?

4. Hoping to _____ a buyer, my brother placed a large sign on the windshield of his car.

5. Once the police realized that the fire was not a(n) _____ act, they called off their criminal investigation.

6. Each time the young performer practiced her music she became more _____ that her concert would be a success.

7. The woman wore makeup to _____ the bruise on her face.

8. As the district attorney described a(n) _____ crime, members of the jury could not hide their feelings of horror.

Pages 38–65 (cont.)

Questions:

1. Why does Slim think that George and Lennie's relationship is unusual?

2. Why does Carlson want to shoot Candy's old dog?

3. Why does Slim condone Carlson's desire to shoot the dog?

4. What is Candy's reaction to the killing of his dog?

5. Why doesn't George want to consider a lasting relationship with a woman?

6. Why does George allow Candy to become part of their dream to own a farm? How does this affect the reality of their dream?

7. Why is Lennie reluctant to fight Curley? How does the result of this fight between Curley and Lennie reveal Lennie's strength?

8. How does Slim save Lennie and George from being fired?

Questions for Discussion:

1. Why do you think George tells Slim why he and Lennie had to leave Weed?

2. Why do you think the author had Carlson explain in detail how he would go about shooting Candy's dog? Do you believe there is justification in ending the life of a living creature once it is no longer productive?

3. Why do you think George and Lennie "jumped as though they had been caught doing something reprehensible" when they were interrupted in their talk about a farm of their own? Given their present reality, what is so reprehensible about their dreaming their dream?

4. Why do you think Slim is considered the most rational, trusted person in the bunkhouse?

5. In your opinion, is George's dream meant to seem realistic? If the men were to buy their own place, could they sustain it?

Literary Devices:

I. *Symbolism*—A symbol in literature is an object, person, or event that represents an idea or set of ideas. What does Carlson's pistol and the loaded shell symbolize?

_____

_____

Pages 38–65 (cont.)

II. *Motif*—What parts of George's story have become a motif?

_____

_____

_____

Why do you think Lennie needs to hear the story repeatedly, and why does George agree to repeat it?

_____

_____

_____

Writing Activity:

Each one of the characters in the story has a different reaction to Lennie. Imagine you are one of the characters and write a description of Lennie from your point of view. Compare your description with those of others who are reading this book.

PAGES 66 - 83

Vocabulary: Use the context to select the best meaning of the underlined word in each of the following sentences. Circle the letter of the answer you choose.

1. James was such a proud, <u>aloof</u> man that people kept their distance.

   a. gregarious   b. athletic   c. haughty   d. scholarly

2. The corner of the room remained hidden in shadow because the single light suspended from the ceiling cast a <u>meager</u> yellow light.

   a. scanty   b. ebullient   c. glowing   d. hazy

3. The victim's parents stared <u>contemptuously</u> at the person who had injured their daughter.

   a. tragically   b. hurriedly   c. respectfully   d. disdainfully

4. After months of therapy, Jill felt her <u>ego</u> was strong enough to face job interviews.

   a. other   b. self   c. relative   d. spouse

5. After working out and dieting for months, the runner's body appeared strong and <u>lean</u>.

   a. attractive   b. overweight   c. robust   d. thin

6. A <u>scowl</u> appeared on the man's face as soon as he saw the dented fender on his new car.

   a. birthmark   b. smile   c. frown   d. lesion

7. The little girl was so shy that she hid behind her mother and <u>averted</u> her eyes each time someone spoke to her.

   a. turned towards   b. turned away   c. blinked rapidly   d. closed tightly

Questions:

1. Why does Crooks strongly defend his territory?

2. Why didn't Crooks' background prepare him for the isolation he experiences on the ranch?

3. Why does Crooks force Lennie to imagine life without George?

4. What problem does Curley's wife have in common with Crooks?

5. What is Curley's wife really threatening when she yells at Crooks, "Listen, Nigger. You know what I can do if you open your trap"? How effective is this threat?

6. Why does Crooks pretend that he doesn't want to live on the ranch with Candy, George, and Lennie?

Pages 66–83 (cont.)

Questions for Discussion:

1. Do you think Crooks is unnecessarily cruel to Lennie when he tries to keep him out of his room and when he wants Lennie to imagine being without George? Is there any justification for his behavior?

2. As the question of whether the men will have their land is bandied back and forth, does the author set up the expectation that their dream will end in success or failure? How have you reached this conclusion?

Literary Device: Symbolism

What does the rattle of halter chains in Crooks' room symbolize?

_____

_____

Literary Element: Theme

A theme in a work of literature is an implied statement about life, an idea that is central to the work, or a lesson to be learned. One important theme in this novel is alienation or isolation. How does each of the characters reveal this theme? How does the conversation between Curley and Crooks further illustrate this theme?

Writing Activity:

Write about a time when you felt isolated or alienated from those around you. What kind of treatment did you receive that created this sense of isolation? Why did others perceive you as being different? How did you deal with the situation?

PAGES 84–98

Vocabulary: Analogies are word equations in which the first pair of words has the same relationship as the second pair of words. For example, YOUTH is to AGE as TOIL is to REST. Both pairs of words are opposites. Use the words in the Word Box to complete the following analogies.

```
                        WORD BOX
        confide      contorted      whimper
        console      earnestly
```

1. INITIATE is to CONCLUDE as IRRITATE is to _____.

2. PURSUE is to GOAL as _____ is to SECRET.

3. _____ is to FRIVOLOUSLY as AGGRESSIVE is to COMPLACENT.

4. BODY is to CONVULSED as FACE is to _____.

5. SOB is to _____ as GUFFAW is to GIGGLE.

Questions:

1. What does Curley's wife have in common with the men in the bunkhouse?

2. Why does Lennie kill Curley's wife?

3. Why does George have Candy pretend to discover the body a little later than he actually did?

4. How does the death of Curley's wife affect Lennie, George, Candy, and Curley?

Questions for Discussion:

1. Why do you think the author has Lennie talk to himself and to Curley's wife about the way the puppy died?

2. Do you think Curley's wife is guilty of enticing Lennie and thereby bringing about her own death?

3. Why do you think the author reveals a sharp contrast between the appearance of Curley's wife in life and in death?

Pages 84 - 98 (cont.)

Literary Element: Plot

The plot of a novel is its sequence of events. Usually, the events rise to a climax, or moment of greatest drama. Then, there is a resolution and conclusion. This can be shown graphically as follows:

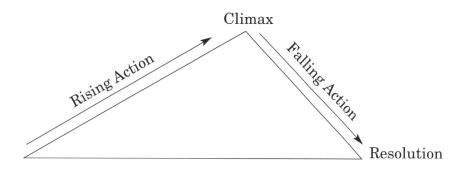

What events provide the rising action?

_____

_____

_____

What event is the climax?

_____

_____

What do you predict will be the resolution?

_____

_____

Writing Activity:

Write about a time when you knew that one of your goals would never be realized. Describe your imagined goal and tell why your hopes were dashed. Have you redirected your goal or do you still have bad feelings about this disappointment?

PAGES 99–107

Vocabulary: Draw a line from each word on the left to its definition on the right. Then use the numbered words to fill in the blanks in the sentences below.

1. belligerent
2. monotonous
3. retorted
4. woodenly
5. mottled

a. answered
b. awkwardly; stiffly
c. hostile; angry
d. speckled
e. unvarying

. . . .

1. Not wanting to reveal his emotions, George responded _____ to questions about Lennie.

2. The constant repetition of the story about the farm was _____ to everyone but Lennie.

3. By the pool among the _____ sycamores, a pleasant shade had fallen.

4. Slim _____ angrily when Curley was critical of the farmhands.

5. A _____ personality such as Curley's was bound to end up in a serious fight.

Questions:

1. How much time passes in the course of this novel?

2. How does the author reveal Lennie's feelings and his fears?

3. When George finds Lennie in the bushes, Lennie insists that he go through the usual motions of scolding him and telling him how things are with them. What effect does this produce?

4. How does Lennie's death compare to the way Candy's dog was killed?

Questions for Discussion:

1. Of the several deaths that were reported in the course of this novel, why do you think the author had the reader "witness" Lennie's death?

2. Do you think George could have solved his problem with Lennie in any other way? Do you believe his solution was cruel? Was it necessary? How do you think the author wanted you to feel when Lennie was shot?

3. The book might have ended as Slim and George walked toward the highway. Instead, Steinbeck added a coda with Carlson saying, "What the hell ya suppose is eatin' them two guys"? Why do you think this was added?

Pages 99–107 (cont.)

Literary Element: Setting

The setting of a work of fiction is the time and place in which the events occur. Notice the setting of the last section, as revealed in the opening page, and compare it to the setting as described in the first few pages of the book. What is similar and what has changed? Why do you think the author has ended the book close to where it began?

_____

_____

_____

_____

Writing Activity:

What future does Steinbeck suggest for George? Will he ever have his farm? Will he live a more carefree life without Lennie? Will he always be a migrant farm worker? Write another chapter for the book in which you project George's future life.

CLOZE ACTIVITY

The following passage has been taken from page 84 of the book. Read it through completely. Then fill in each blank with a word that makes sense. When you have finished, you may compare your language with that of the author.

One end of the great barn was piled high with new hay and over the pile hung the four-taloned Jackson fork suspended from its pulley. The hay came down like a mountain _____ [1] to the other end of the barn, _____ [2] there was a level place as yet _____ [3] with the new crop. At the sides _____ [4] feeding racks were visible, and between the _____ [5] the heads of horses could be seen.

_____ [6] was Sunday afternoon. The resting horses nibbled _____ [7] remaining wisps of hay, and they stamped _____ [8] feet and they bit the wood of _____ [9] mangers and rattled the halter chains. The _____ [10] sun sliced in through the cracks of _____ [11] barn walls and lay in bright lines _____ [12] the hay. There was the buzz of _____ [13] in the air, the lazy afternoon humming. _____ [14] outside came the clang of horseshoes on _____ [15] playing peg and the shouts of men, _____, [16] encouraging, jeering. But in the barn it _____ [17] quiet and humming and lazy and warm. _____ [18] Lennie was in the barn, and Lennie _____ [19] in the hay beside a packing case _____ [20] a manger in the end of the _____ [21] that had not been filled with hay. _____ [22] sat in the hay and looked at _____ [23] little dead puppy that lay in front _____ [24] him. Lennie looked at it for a long time, and then he put out his huge hand and stroked it, stroked it clear from one end to the other.

POST-READING ACTIVITIES

1. Return to the list of motifs you began as you were reading pages 1–16 of the book. Add any motifs that you may have missed. Is there any connection among the motifs? Which do you think are most important? Why do you think the author used these motifs?

2. Aristotle defined tragedy as a play about a basically good person, important to society, who suffers a fall brought about by something in his or her nature, provoking the emotions of pity and fear in the audience.
   - Based on the above definition, show how the novel *Of Mice and Men* is a tragedy.
   - Based on this definition show how it is not a tragedy.

3. Do you think it is an oversight on Steinbeck's part that Curley's wife was never given a name? If not, what are some of the reasons the author might have chosen to leave this character nameless?

4. Each section of the novella could be a scene in a play. Describe how the stage would be set and the action portrayed in each segment of the novella.

5. The characters in *Of Mice and Men* utter racially derogatory phrases. Why do you think they use this language? Given the context of the story, are these terms necessary? Is there any evidence to suggest that Steinbeck shares his characters' bigoted views of minorities?

6. Loneliness is a major theme in the novel. It is expressed in many of the things that the characters say and do. Show how loneliness is a part of the life of each of the following characters:
   - Crooks
   - Candy
   - Lennie
   - George
   - Curley's wife

7. The literary device of foreshadowing, or giving clues in advance of an important event, is used effectively in this novel. Identify as many of the incidents and bits of dialogue as you can that provide clues to the outcome.

8. Under ordinary circumstances, a man like Lennie, who was simple-minded, unattractive, and capable of accidental violence, would not be an object of sympathy. Review the novel to ascertain the many ways in which Steinbeck was able to evoke the reader's sympathy for Lennie. If the reader did not have compassion for him, how would the effect of the ending be different?

Post-Reading Activities (cont.)

9. At one point in the story, there are four characters daydreaming about life on their own ranch: George, Lennie, Candy, and Crooks. Each of these characters is in some way "broken" or incomplete. Discuss the ways in which each of these characters has lost his dignity.

10. This novel portrays several killings:
    - Slim drowning his dog's pups
    - Carlson killing Candy's dog
    - Lennie killing the pup
    - Lennie killing Curley's wife
    - George killing Lennie

    Compare the motives for each of these killings and determine whether each was justified. Why do you think the author depicted the killing of animals before the killing of humans? Were the moral issues the same or different?

SUGGESTIONS FOR FURTHER READING

Blinn, William. *Brian's Song*. Random House.

* Byars, Betsy. *The Pinballs*. HarperCollins.

* Cormier, Robert. *The Chocolate War*. Random House.

Fairbairn, Ann. *That Man Cartwright*. Random House.

* Hunt, Irene. *The Lottery Rose*. Random House.

* _____. *No Promises in the Wind*. Random House.

Hutchinson, R.C. *A Child Possessed*. HarperCollins.

* Jones, Ron. *The Acorn People*. Random House.

Killilea, Marie. *Karen*. Random House.

* Keyes, Daniel. *Flowers for Algernon*. Random House.

* Levoy, Myron. *Alan and Naomi*. HarperCollins.

McCarthy, Paul. *John Steinbeck*. Contimum.

* Orwell, George. *Animal Farm*. New American Library.

* Spinelli, Jerry. *Maniac Magee*. HarperCollins.

* Swarthout, Glendon. *Bless the Beasts and Children*. Simon & Schuster.

Wartski, Maureen. *My Brother is Special*. New American Library.

Welty, Eudora. *The Ponder Heart*. Harcourt.

* Wright, Richard. *Black Boy*. HarperCollins.

Zindel, Paul. *Confessions of a Teen-Age Baboon*. Random House.

* _____. *The Pigman*. HarperCollins.

Some Other Books by John Steinbeck

Cannery Row. Penguin.

East of Eden. Penguin

The Grapes of Wrath. Penguin.

Moon is Down. Penguin.

* *The Pearl*. Penguin.

* *The Red Pony*. Penguin.

Tortilla Flat. Penguin.

Travels With Charley in Search of America. Penguin.

Winter of Our Discontent. Penguin.

* NOVEL-TIES Study Guides are available for these titles.

ANSWER KEY

Pages 1–16

Vocabulary: 1. c 2. g 3. d 4. f 5. a 6. b 7. e; 1. morosely 2. emerge 3. dejected 4. lumbered 5. contemplated 6. imperiously 7. recumbent

Questions: 1. Lennie is immediately seen as a large, hulking adult who lacks good sense. George worries that he will drink too much impure water and become sick again. He is first likened to a playful puppy, then to an imitative child. He is unable to retain simple information. We are left with the impression that he is not in full control of all his mental faculties. 2. George regards Lennie as both a burden that was thrust upon him and a responsibility he assumed willingly. In many ways, George acts like a parent, while Lennie is the loving, but simple, child. 3. Lennie and George are headed to a ranch in Soledad. They have just left a ranch up north in Weed where Lennie had innocently tried to touch the fabric on a girl's dress. She screamed and George and Lennie left quickly to avoid problems. 4. As ranch hands, Lennie and George generally follow the work on a seasonal basis. Lennie also gets himself into trouble so often that it is impossible to stay in one place for long. 5. Lennie has killed mice and he may well have assaulted a girl in Weed. This behavior was the result of Lennie's childlike interest in soft (mice) and pretty (the girl's dress) objects. Any harm done was the result of his inability to respond appropriately. 6. George warns Lennie not to say a word to the boss, so that the rancher won't find out that he's mentally deficient. Also, he establishes a place that Lennie can escape to in case he runs into trouble. These precautions suggest that George feels history will probably repeat itself and that they will probably have to move on before they can save enough money to afford a place of their own.

Pages 17–37

Vocabulary: 1. scoff–mock; jeer 2. ominously–in a way that threatens danger 3. plaintively–sorrowfully; sadly 4. majesty–stately dignity 5. profound–deep; penetrating 6. precede–go before 7. liniment–soothing salve to apply to the skin

Questions: 1. Crooks is at the bottom of the bunkhouse hierarchy because he is a black man. 2. Candy always "sugar coats" situations to make them more acceptable. For example, he explains to George that the presence of insecticide powder near George's bedside has more to do with how meticulous Whitey (the bed's former inhabitant) was about personal hygiene than with the actual presence of lice. 3. The boss thinks it is unusual for one man to take care of another unless he has ulterior motives, such as cheating him out of his earnings. 4. George lies because it provides a more plausible explanation of Lennie's inability to engage in normal conversations and activities. He also does it to protect their jobs. One final reason he might lie is to give everyone fair warning about Lennie's deficiency so that if he slips up, others will judge him more leniently. 5. As the boss's son, Curley cannot be fired for any offense. As a man of small stature, he seems to handle his insecurity with a bravado that includes instigating fights with larger men, like Lennie. If Lennie wins or loses such a fight, it would cost George and Lennie their jobs. 6. Curley's attractive and flirtatious wife may attempt to seduce Lennie. His predilection for anything that is soft to touch may cause him to succumb; thus, placing himself and George at risk. 7. Slim is at the top of the bunkhouse hierarchy. As a jerkline skinner on the ranch, he is a master at a specialized skill. He is admired for his skill, his knowledge, and his low-key demeanor. 8. The ranch hands seem to live in a world lacking close human relationships. Slim's remark suggests admiration for the devotion Lennie and George have for one another. The boss, on the other hand, spoke cynically, suggesting that George wants to rob Lennie of his pay.

Pages 38 – 65

Vocabulary: 1. d 2. e 3. f 4. g 5. a 6. c 7. b 8. h; 1. cautious 2. entranced 3. sarcasm 4. attract 5. deliberate 6. confident 7. conceal 8. reprehensible

Questions: 1. Slim thinks that it is odd to find two men traveling together, particularly because ranch hands tend to be loners. He is also surprised that a bright man, such as George, would have a simple man, such as Lennie, as a companion. 2. Carlson wants to shoot Candy's old dog because he is troubled by the dog's odor and obvious suffering. Not considering Candy's attachment to the animal, he wants to end the dog's misery and his own discomfort. 3. Slim condones Carlson's desire to shoot the dog because he thinks that it is merciful to put a fellow creature out of its misery. 4. Candy is distraught about the loss of the dog, a longtime companion whom he loved. He also wonders if he will fall prey to the philosophy of eliminating a creature once it is no longer useful. 5. George believes that a woman would complicate and ruin his life. He prefers leaving women alone or indulging in a one-night stand. 6. George allows Candy to join them in their dream for the future because he has saved $350, while George has only $10. Candy's money could make the

dream possible. 7. Lennie is reluctant to fight Curley because of George's repeated warnings. Lennie crushes Curley's hand without much effort. This indicates that Lennie does not know his own tremendous strength and cannot control it. 8. Slim saves Lennie and George from being fired by warning Curley that he must say it was a machine and not Lennie who crushed his hand.

Pages 66 – 83

Vocabulary: 1. c 2. a 3. d 4. b 5. d 6. c 7. b

Questions: 1. Crooks has a much more circumscribed existence than the others. He is excluded from their activities and living quarters. The only way to ensure that his private areas don't become a playground for the racial rules that prevail elsewhere is to keep them off limits. 2. In some ways Crooks was not prepared for a life of exclusion because his father was a land owner and as a child he enjoyed the freedom to play with white children. He just assumed that this was natural. He never could understand why his father always objected to it. And even as he grew older, he never really understood just how isolating his race could be until he realized that he was the only black man on the ranch. 3. Crooks forces Lennie to imagine life without George because he wants someone else to know how it feels to be utterly alone. 4. Like Crooks, Curley's wife is desperately lonely. She regards her husband as a fool and he is certainly not a companion for her. 5. Curley's wife is threatening to yell "rape," thereby getting Crooks lynched. Answers to the last part of the question will vary. 6. Crooks pretends that he doesn't want to live on the ranch with Candy, George, and Lennie because he realizes that even among those who have nothing and nowhere to go, he is still at the bottom of the ladder. He thinks that it is futile to dream of a better life.

Pages 84 – 98

Vocabulary: 1. console 2. confide 3. earnestly 4. contorted 5. whimper

Questions: 1. Curley's wife, like the men in the bunkhouse, lives in a world of hopeless, unfulfilled dreams. Her imagined world of success and glamour parallels the men's dream of a farm of their own. 2. Lennie becomes confused and alarmed when Curley's wife tells him to stop stroking her hair. As in the past under these circumstances, he holds on tighter than is necessary. This makes Curley's wife scream and Lennie accidentally breaks her neck trying to quiet her. 3. George has Candy pretend to discover the body later than he actually did because he doesn't want the other men to think that he had anything to do with the murder. 4. In the aftermath of the death of Curley's wife, Lennie is upset because he knows he will never realize his dream of tending rabbits; George and Candy fully understand that the farm will never be theirs. Their sorrow is not for Curley's wife, but for the loss of their dreams. Curley reacts to his wife's death with anger, wanting violent revenge. He does not show any other signs of grief.

Pages 99 – 107

Vocabulary: 1. c 2. e 3. a 4. b 5. d; 1. woodenly 2. monotonous 3. mottled 4. retorted 5. belligerent

Questions: 1. The events of the novel take place in less than a year—from spring to autumn. 2. In the segment of fantasy in which Lennie talks to an imagined Aunt Clara and a rabbit, the author is able to externalize Lennie's feelings and his fears. 3. This scene reminds the reader of other times when these same words were spoken. During these other times, there was a sense of hopefulness and the refrain conveyed the value of their companionship. Now George can barely utter the words. 4. Both Lennie and Candy's dog were shot in the back of the head "for their own good."